Explore
GRASSLAND
HABITATS
with Ji-Young

Charlotte Reed

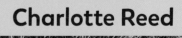

Lerner Publications ◆ Minneapolis

T0016546

There are many habitats to explore!

In the Sesame Street® Habitats series, young readers will take a tour of eight habitats. Join your friends from *Sesame Street* as they learn about these different habitats where animals live, sleep, and find food and water.

Sincerely,
The Editors at Sesame Workshop

Table of Contents

WHAT IS A HABITAT?

Let's explore habitats! A habitat is a place where animals live and can find water, food, and a place to sleep. A grassland is a type of habitat.

A habitat is a home for animals and plants.

Only a little rain falls in grassland habitats, but they still get enough rain for grass to grow.

LET'S LOOK AT GRASSLAND HABITATS

Grassland habitats have different names depending on what part of the world they're in. There are temperate and tropical grasslands.

Every continent except Antarctica has grasslands!

Temperate grasslands are mild. That means the weather doesn't get too hot or too cold.

Pronghorn antelopes live in temperate grasslands. They run really fast!

In North America, grasslands are called prairies. Prairies are temperate. Bison live on prairies and graze. That means they eat grass.

Bison run fast and jump high fences. Bison are good swimmers too!

There are not many trees in grassland habitats, so some animals, like prairie dogs, live underground.

Steppes are another type of temperate grassland. They are in Asia and Europe. Steppes are home to saiga antelopes.

Saiga antelopes travel far distances.

Saiga antelopes graze on grasses.

In South America, grasslands are called pampas. Pampas are temperate grasslands too. These grasslands are home to guanacos. Guanacos have long eyelashes to help protect their eyes from dust and wind.

A baby guanaco is called a chulengo.

19

Tropical grasslands are warm all year. Africa and Australia have tropical grassland habitats.

These grasslands are called savannas.

21

Kangaroos hop across Australian savannas. Kangaroos use their strong tails for balance while jumping. Baby kangaroos are called joeys.

In African savannas, an elephant's large ears help keep it cool in the hot sun. Elephants also keep cool by spraying water on their backs with their trunks.

I wear sunglasses and a hat on sunny days!

Grasslands are home to many different animals all over the world.

Which animal would you like to learn more about?

I want to learn about all the animals!

CAN YOU GUESS?

1. Which one of these pictures shows a grassland?

A

B

2. Which one of these animals lives in a grassland?

A

B

Glossary

graze: when animals, such as bison or saiga antelopes, eat grass in a field

habitat: a place where animals live and can find water, food, and a place to sleep

temperate: an area that has a cold season, a warm season, and rain all year

tropical: an area that is warm all year and has seasons when it rains a lot and seasons when it doesn't rain very much

Can You Guess? Answers

1. A
2. B

Read More

Mazzarella, Kerri Lee. *Grassland Biome*. Coral Springs, FL: Seahorse Publishing, 2022.

Reed, Charlotte. *Explore Ocean Habitats with Elmo*. Minneapolis: Lerner Publications, 2024.

Sabelko, Rebecca. *Grassland Animals*. Minneapolis: Bellwether Media, 2023.

Photo Acknowledgments

Images used: Tetra Images/Getty Images, p. 1; DouglasOlivares/Getty Images, p. 5; JurgaR/Getty Images, p. 6; Foto4440/Getty Images, p. 8–9; W. Perry Conway/Getty Images, p. 10; Utah-based Photographer Ryan Houston/Getty Images, p. 11; Cheri Alguire/Getty Images (background, top right), p. 13; Cris Cantón/Getty Images, p. 14; VictorTyakht/Getty Images, p. 17; Foto4440/Getty Images, p. 18; encrier/Getty Images, p. 19; AlexanderXXI/Getty Images, p. 20; robertharding/Alamy, p. 22; vannoyphotography/Shutterstock, p. 25; imageBROKER/Alamy (background), p. 26; Gabriel Rojo/Alamy (left), p. 26; vzmaze/Getty Images (right), p. 26; Paul Tessier/Shutterstock, p. 27; Chris Moody/Shutterstock (left), p. 28; Cavan-Images/Shutterstock (right), p. 28; Michel VIARD/Getty Images (left), p. 29; Frank Fichtmueller/Shutterstock (right), p. 29.
Cover: Darrell Gulin/Getty Images; Maciej Czekajewski/Shutterstock; StanislavBeloglazov/Shutterstock; Frank Fichtmueller/Shutterstock.

Index

For my sister Amber and my nephew Nate. May your hearts and library always be full.

Lerner Publications Company
An imprint of Lerner Publishing Group, Inc.
241 First Avenue North
Minneapolis, MN 55401 USA

For reading levels and more information, look up this title at www.lernerbooks.com.

Main body text set in Mikado. Typeface provided by HVD.

Editor: Amber Ross **Designer:** Laura Otto Rinne
Lerner team: Martha Kranes, Sue Marquis

Library of Congress Cataloging-in-Publication Data

Names: Reed, Charlotte, 1997- author.
Title: Explore grassland habitats with Ji-Young / Charlotte Reed.
Description: Minneapolis : Lerner Publications, [2024] | Series: Sesame Street habitats | Includes bibliographical references and index. | Audience: Ages 4-8 | Audience: Grades K-1 | Summary: "Grasslands are found all over the world. Come along with Ji-Young and her Sesame Street friends as they travel across the globe to learn about the animals and characteristics of grassland habitats"– Provided by publisher.
Identifiers: LCCN 2023004527 (print) | LCCN 2023004528 (ebook) | ISBN 9798765604250 (lib. bdg.) | ISBN 9798765617540 (epub)
Subjects: LCSH: Grassland animals—Habitations—Juvenile literature. | Grassland ecology—Juvenile literature. | BISAC: JUVENILE NONFICTION / Science & Nature / Environmental Science & Ecosystems
Classification: LCC QL115.3 .R44 2024 (print) | LCC QL115.3 (ebook) | DDC 591.74—dc23/eng/20230420

LC record available at https://lccn.loc.gov/2023004527
LC ebook record available at https://lccn.loc.gov/2023004528

ISBN 979-8-7656-2486-9 (pbk.)

Manufactured in the United States of America
1-1009562-51412-6/15/2023